Say One Again

Compiled by Graham Spicer

ISBN 0 85346 198 8
© The United Reformed Church, 2000

Published by the United Reformed Church
86 Tavistock Place, London WC1H 9RT

All rights reserved. No part of this publication may be
reproduced, stored in a retrieval system, or transmitted in
any form or by any means, electronic, mechanical,
photocopying, recording, or otherwise without prior
permission of the publisher.

Produced by Communications and Editorial, Graphics Office

Printed by Healeys Printers, Unit 10, The Sterling Complex,
Farthing Road, Ipswich, Suffolk IP1 5AP

Preface

Say One Again

Preaching in the parish church one Week of Prayer for Christian Unity, I was delighted to find amongst all the usual liturgical clutter in the Rector's stall a copy of the *Prayer Handbook* that I had given my clergy friends one Christmas. It was battered and well-thumbed, and folded open for the previous Sunday in the Church's year. I was not alone in treasuring it as a resource!

The *Prayer Handbook* began as the *Watchers Prayer Union* handbook, first published by the London Missionary Society in 1895, and which continued to be published by the LMS and its successors until 1985. Though the structures, methods and relationships of mission have evolved almost beyond recognition, the need for inspiring and informing prayer remains as strong as ever. The United Reformed Church continues to produce the *Prayer Handbook* in co-operation with the English-speaking members of the Council for World Mission.

These "meditations, prayers, stories, even the occasional sermon," as one *Prayer Handbook* editor described them, are taken from the first ten years of the Church's stewardship. The choice is my own; these still work for me and I hope they will for you. They are arranged around the themes of the Liturgical Year, the Church, the World and its People.

Preface

The working title for this compilation was
Now That's What I Call Prayer Volume 106 - but
Say One Again echoes the title of the 1990 edition
with its cheerfully confident cover artwork.

Thank you Francis Brienen, Tony Burnham,
Kate Compston, Graham Cook, Muriel Garrow,
David Greenwood, Janet Hargis, David Jenkins,
Janet Lees, Kate McIlhagga, Jean Mortimer,
Stephen Orchard, Bernard Thorogood and
Bob Warwicker for sharing your inspiration
and insight; and *Prayer Handbook* editors
Edmund Banyard, Kate Compston and
Graham Cook for your skill and judgement.

Graham Spicer
Stratford-upon-Avon
March 2000

Advent

Can't wait

Romans 8:16-28

*"What does Advent mean?" the minister asked the children
in the church. "Can't wait," a little girl answered.*

God of promise,
this is the time of "can't wait". In the groaning of creation,
in floods and rainbows, we long to know your promise.

This is the time of "can't wait". In the love and the challenge
of the people we meet, we long to hear your good news.

This is the time of "can't wait". In the loneliness and hatred,
in the darkness of this world, we long to see your light.

This is the time of "can't wait".
In the depth of our being,
in the forgotten corners of our heart, we long to feel
your presence.

God of promise and truth, in this time of "can't wait"
we are still and wait …

Use this moment of silence
to prepare our hearts.
Use this moment to make us wakeful,
that we might recognise the signs of your coming and
know you.

Francis Brienen

Advent

Expecting

Malachi 3:1-5

Lord
we confess
that our expectations of your coming
are often warped and twisted;
faltering faith and stubborn selfishness combine to produce
a web of tangled hopes.

We dream of a coming which will satisfy our cravings
for status, popularity and power: a macho-Messiah to bolster
our flagging egos; a Santa-Claus Saviour to fulfil our need
for comfort.

We remain frustrated and fearful, still hungry for your living
bread and thirsty for your refreshing waters.

Unravel our conflicting expectations and uncover our deeper
longings; not for gods in our own likeness nor repetitions of
former heroes, but for a new and living experience of your
presence in the world.

Then who can abide the day of your coming?

Lord
let us look upon your coming
as a time for
raising up those who are cast down,
drying the tears of those who weep
and filling a saddened world with unexpected joy. Let it be a
day of jubilee celebrating your power to transform human life
into all you expected and hoped it would be.

David Jenkins

Advent

Messengers

2 Peter 1:19 - 2:5

We light a light for the past,
and give thanks for the messenger of Jordan, proclaiming
the advent of someone greater than he, urging all people to
prepare their hearts.
We rejoice that through the ages
the message has brought hope and joy.

We light a light for the present
and give thanks for the messengers of today, their message
like a lamp shining in a dark place, calling us to watch and pray.
We rejoice that God is always faithful
and keeps calling for us.

God of our yesterday,
our today
and our tomorrow,
we light our candles
as we wait for the light of the morning star. Help us to discern
your presence and to follow in the Way of the truth. Teach us
to live in expectation, that everything we do today is done in
the certainty of your Day dawning.

Francis Brienen

Advent

Firing the Faithful

Luke 4:14-21

You ask me why
I do not tear the skies apart and come down to make the
mountains shake and the nations tremble?

But see what happens
when I slip gently into the world through a stable door in
Bethlehem and become a common carpenter in Nazareth.

They let me read the lesson in the synagogue,
the one about bringing good news to the poor, freedom to
captives, the healing of the blind, and liberty to the oppressed.
They liked that, especially when I said
that it was coming true that very day.
For it seemed to support their suppositions
about their unique claims to have a hold on God.
But when I started to unpack it
and pointed out that poor meant all the poor in all the world,
like the widow of Zarephath, a foreigner, and that healing
was available to everyone in all the world, like Naaman,
the Syrian, a gentile; what a riot that started.
The nations might not have trembled at my coming,
but my own village did.
The mountains did not shake,
but the people in their anger did.
For I undermined their prejudice
and turned upside down their understanding of the world.

So perhaps it is as well
that my coming to you was not more dramatic than it was:
for the response to my gentle, unobtrusive entry was hard
enough to take.

Graham Cook

Advent

Steadfast and encouraging God,
warm the hearts of your faithful people
who joyfully work that love may be shown
in the joyless places where others are out in the cold:
in shanty towns and cardboard cities,
in concrete jungles and overcrowded night shelters,
in alcohol and drug dependence centres,
in half-way houses for discharged prisoners and patients.

Fire the protest of your faithful people
who tirelessly work that right may prevail
in the corridors of power, where need is cold-shouldered
or kept waiting, tied up in the endless red tape of faceless
committees chiefly concerned with cutting back.

Shine through the eyes of your faithful people
who joyfully wait for your day of salvation
in the godless places where no one calls on your name,
where faith is proscribed and protest silenced, where freedom
is shackled and justice turns a blind eye.

Re-kindle in all of us the spirit of Jesus,
who stood up to be counted in his own community, who
proclaimed your freedom in his local church. Call us to be
faithful in our daily living to the prophecy which he fulfilled
in his day.

Jean Mortimer

Christmas

God in Time and Eternity

Zechariah 2:10-13

Let us keep silence
in the presence of God who has come from a holy dwelling
place to a humble stable, to be at home with us.

Let us keep silence
in the presence of God who has come to us from the safety
of a woman's womb, to run the risk of human living.

Let us keep silence
in the presence of God who has come to us in the pain of
labour in the blood of birth,
to proclaim a new heaven and a new earth.

Let us keep silence
in the presence of God who has spoken to us in the startled
cry of infant lungs sucking in the cold night air.

Let us keep silence
in the presence of God who has spoken to us in the gurgling
contentment of a baby, fed and warmed at a mother's breast.

Let us keep silence
in the presence of God, who lies wide open to us, helpless and
dependent in a woman's arms.

Let us keep silence
before the wonder and the mystery of God in human flesh,
God in touch,
God in time and eternity.

Jean Mortimer

Christmas

Touching the Ground

Isaiah 49:7-13

In the moontime of the winter, when the sun redly rises; in the moontime of the winter, when the trees starkly stretch, then, O Christ, you come: softly as a gently falling snowflake, with the lusty energy of a newborn boy, the blood and pain of your coming, staining the distant horizon.

In the frost of the starlight,
when the sun gives way to moon,
in the frost of the starlight,
when the earth is turned to stone, then, O Christ you come: slowly as the rhythm of the seasons, quickly as the rush of cradling waters, worshipped by the wise, adored by the humble, the ecstatic joy of your coming, heralding songs of peace.

Into the world of refugee and soldier,
the soles of your feet have touched the ground. Into the world of banker and beggar, the soles of your feet have touched the ground. Into the world of Jew and Arab, the soles of your feet have touched the ground.

Walk with us Saviour of the poor, be a light on our way, travel beside the weary, fill the broken hearted with hope and heal the nations, that all may walk in the light of the glory of God.

Kate McIlhagga

Christmas

'He came to dwell amongst us'.

John 1. 14-18

The literal translation is that he came to pitch his tent amongst us.
It is an expression often used about the presence of God.

It was in the tent, pitched outside the camp, that Moses met with
God. It is in the new Jerusalem of Revelation that God pitches his
tent and is with his people.

God cannot be tied down, contained and confined to one place.
His tent is pitched outside the camp and when they catch up with
him, he moves on and pitches it in another place. He is a God of
no permanent address, no abiding place.

Even when they try to tie him down by turning the fabric of his tent
into stone and surrounding it with flying buttresses he still manages
to keep on the move.

They built a cathedral in Calcutta to pin him down in the midst of
Empire so that he could see that it was good and extend his blessing
on it forever. Young men came to its doors and were turned away
because they were 'native'. But God could not be tied down even
by such a weight of stone. One of the 'native' young men who was
turned away from worship lived to become Bishop of the Diocese.
One of his young men became Provost Subir Biswas under whose
care the barn-like building was turned into a barn, a warehouse for
aid materials. The congregation had to find its way towards the
altar by narrow alleyways between towering walls of rice sacks,
flour bags and blankets.

Even when the tent was turned to stone, he moved it.
The word that had become a dead letter became flesh and lived
amongst us.

He is come with us to dwell,
Our prince, our guide, our love, our Lord.
And he is called Emmanuel,
God present with his world restored.

Graham Cook

Christmas

Living God
though no one has seen you we can know about you
through Jesus born of woman.

We worship you
for though you are holy you became one of us
as Jesus born of woman.

We praise you
for though all powerful you were as weak as a baby
in Jesus born of woman.

In your mercy, God
forgive us for disabling your incarnation
by separating Mary from all other mothers.

We are glad for her likeness to them, carrying her baby in her
body, letting him go when the time was right, feeding and
nursing him, and loving him tenderly.

We praise you for the influence of Mary
when we see all that Jesus became;
strength shown in weakness, authority shown in impotence,
majesty shown in compassion, and love shown in self-sacrifice.

So God, let our praise and adoration, in gratitude for all that
Mary, was reverberate throughout time
in the name of Jesus born of woman.

Tony Burnham

New Year

Son Bright

Jeremiah 31:15-17

The world belongs to God
the earth and all its people. How good and how lovely it
is to live together in unity.
Love and faithfulness meet, justice and peace embrace.
If the Lord's disciples keep silent these stones would
shout aloud.

Almighty One, who brought us through the darkness of sleep
to the bright light of this new day, guide us through this year:
in dark and light, in pain and joy, in snow and sun, through
heartbreak to sonbright; and from today's joyous light bring
us to the guiding light of eternity.

O Christ, who wept over Jerusalem,
hear the cries of Rachel weeping for her children, as women
weep the world over for hope snatched from their arms.
At the gate of the year,
strengthen those
who look back through tears
and forward without hope.
Covenant with those who trust in you.

Holy Spirit giver of new life,
open our mouths in praise,
our hearts to welcome the Christ child and our arms to
embrace the world.

Kate McIlhagga

Epiphany

The Lord is our righteousness

Jeremiah 23:5-8

Not only brought back from Egypt,
not only brought back from exile,
but brought back to wisdom, justice and righteousness.

We thought we knew where to find you; we hardly needed a
star to guide the way, just perseverance and common-sense;
why do you hide yourself away from the powerful and join
the refugees and outcasts, calling us to follow you there?
Wise God, give us wisdom.

We thought we had laid you safe in the manger; we wrapped
you in the thickest sentiment we could find, and stressed how
long ago you came to us; why do you break upon us in our
daily life with messages of peace and goodwill, demanding
that we do something about it?
Just and righteous God, give us justice and righteousness.

You are the God who made childless Sarah laugh,
you took cheating Jacob to father a nation;
Moses, from the household of Pharaoh became a deliverer;
the despised Jeremiah was right in the end.
The weakness of Esther and Rahab and Miriam was turned
into power when your moment came. You scattered your
people in Assyria and Babylon, where they learnt the
greatness of your love; out of what seemed chaos and disaster
your wisdom, justice and righteousness prevailed.

So where else would we expect to find you
but in the ordinary place with the faithful people,
turning the world to your purpose through them.
Bring us to that manger, to that true rejoicing,
which will make wisdom, justice and righteousness alive in us.

Stephen Orchard

Epiphany

World Travellers

Matthew 2:1-12, 19-23

Lord of our journeyings, brighten our way;
Lord of our searching, guide our minds;
Lord of our offerings, show us a child.

Jesus,
born in the world, for the world, may the nations turn to you
in wonder and thankfulness; submitting their tokens of power,
shedding their assertions of wisdom.

May a genuine humility
break into the world of confrontation, of claim and
counter-claim.

May the strongest
glimpse your fragile presence and on bended knee offer
the best.

Hear our prayers for
those who influence world opinion, advisors and spokesmen,
broadcasters and writers, journalists and cartoonists.

Teach us to listen with understanding to those who search for
meaning, those who question and probe for truth, those who
present the claims of nations and of groups - especially those
which are not close to us.

In the name of Jesus, goal of our journey.

David Jenkins

Lent

Choices

Deuteronomy 30:15-20; Matthew 4:1-11

God of the heights and the depths,
we bring to you
those driven into the desert,
those struggling with difficult decisions.

May they choose life

God of the light and the darkness, we bring to you those lost in the mist of drugs or drink, those dazzled by the use of power.

May they choose life

God of the wild beast and the ministering angel, we bring to you those savaged by others' greed, those exhausted by caring for others.

May they feel your healing touch

Christ tempted and triumphant, we bring ourselves to you, tired of difficult choices, anxious about the future, drained by the loss of a loved one.

May we feel your healing touch

May we feel your healing touch, know God's presence in all things and receive the crown of life through the Holy Spirit of compassion.

Kate McIlhagga

Lent

Ahead of us

Luke 9:51; Matthew 28:10 John 14:2

Courageous Lord
You set your face to go to Jerusalem
and steadfastly went ahead of your reluctant disciples.
We thank you
that you continue to go ahead of us into all difficult situations;
wherever there is risk, whenever there is antagonism.
You are already there, ahead of all the enmity, bravely loving.

Gentle Lord
at your resurrection you gave a message to your panic-stricken disciples that you would go ahead of them to Galilee.
We thank you that when we have failed you you continue to go ahead of us to provide a safe meeting place where you lift us up from despair.
You are already there ahead of our disasters, creatively loving.

Living Lord
you told your grieving disciples that you would go ahead to prepare a place for them with God.
We thank you
that you are ahead of us in death, in that most terrifying experience, in the pain and un-knowingness.
You are already there ahead of our fear,
victoriously loving.

Janet Hargis

Holy Week

A Prayer for Passiontide

Lamentations 1:1-14

Compassionate God,
we pray for those who have no land, who work the fields of others, who pick the fruit but do not know its taste.

We pray for those who have no home, who are displaced, uprooted, their homes destroyed by landlords and warlords.

We pray for those who have lost their children, for whom there is no future, their sons taken to war, their daughters sold into slavery.

May their dreams be not broken, May their spirits be not crushed, May their lives be not forgotten.

Instead, break our dreams of 'more', O God, and crush our spirit of greed; we for whom enough is never enough, who do not understand the tears of the poor, whose way of life perpetuates the grip of suffering.

Christ, who went before us,
help us to remember in your passion all those who suffer.
Help us to remember in your passion the promise of justice, the promise of peace, the promise of new life.
You who in your life on earth
cried out to God, pray for us now.

Francis Brienen

Holy Week

Turning upside down

Mark 9:30-37; 11:1-11; 1 Corinthians 1:18-31

Cross-bound Christ
in this Holy Week you question all our human assumptions
about authority and leadership, power and glory.

We look to the Son of the most high God
for splendour.
And you ride into Jerusalem like a jester on a lowly donkey.

We look to the Son of the most high God
for dignity.
And you kneel in the dust like a slave and wash your
followers' feet.

We look to the Son of the most high God
for authority.
And silently you wear your crown upside down so it bruises
your brow, and you bleed.

We look to the Son of the most high God
for command of the situation. And you hang, helpless, on the
gallows-tree and die as an outcast.

Cross-free Christ, unbound,
vindicated by Easter,
help us to see how service, sacrifice, non-violence can be
gloriously powerful in our response to life, as in yours.

Kate Compston

Holy Week

Alive

John 15:5-11

Promises, promises
our lips are filled with promises: tomorrow we'll be different;
tomorrow we'll change.

Don't you despair of us, Lord,
when you hear from our tongues words of peace
whilst in our hands we hold weapons of destruction?
Don't you shake your head in amazement
when our prayers hold the expectation of forgiveness
whilst within our communities there is division and vendetta?

Like iron nails in Roman crosses, drive home the truth, Lord,
made clear in Calvary that Hosannas are not enough;
not enough for peace,
not enough for salvation.
Show us how words are nothing
until they become deeds.
Show us that prayers are nothing
until we start to answer the prayers
which are on the lips of the homeless and the poor.
Show us that the Church is nothing
until her praying hands are washed clean
of prejudice, violence and pride.

Then raise us to life like a new plant emerging from the winter
darkness so that, baptised into Christ's death, we spring up
and in words and deeds bear fruit in plenty:
signs of your Spirit in the world:
your promises come true.

David Jenkins

Holy Week

Why is this Friday called good

Mark 14:32 - 15:4

Those who were there would not have called it that. They had put their hopes in this man. He had reconciled ancient enemies, healed the sick, raised the dead. The blind had been made to see and the deaf to hear. The lame had learned to dance again. Compassion was alive. Peace was possible. Their world was being born again. But then he was nailed to a cross and the sky turned black.

All their hopes were ended. Their dreams were shattered. It was all an illusion. They might have known. He could not win. How could he? One man against the viciousness of the world. One man's love against the vested interests of political and economic might. They smashed him to pieces. So much for dreams.

We know how they felt. Young men still fight over the land he lived in. In other places shoppers are bombed, worshippers are murdered on their way home from church. Young flesh is crucified upon the pride of nations. Young bodies are ruined by drugs, old ones with drink. Minds are manipulated, children are cold. Mothers go hungry and fathers are imprisoned for their political opinions. This is a time when might is right, when viciousness wins, power is Lord.

But look again at that cross. They take away his freedom. They spit in his face. They put a crown of thorns on his head. They beat his body. They push a spear into his side. They take away everything they can touch and many things they cannot. But they cannot defeat his love. That could not be taken away. Love won.

If he had come down from the cross love would not have won. Fear would have won. Pain would have won. The armed might of the occupying power would have won. The conniving sophistry of the religious hierarchy would have won. But none of them did win. Love won.

That is why Friday is good.

Graham Cook

Holy Week

Christ's emptiness and ours

Jesus, empty and alone in Gethsemane's night,
weary of the world and its hollow hosannas,
worn down by the constant demands of the crowd,
worn out by the struggle to make sense of God's will, tired,
tense, tormented by self-doubt, let down by friends who
would not watch with you, betrayed by a loveless kiss,
defended by an empty gesture, disowned by the one who had
boasted of loyalty, you drained to the dregs the cup of human
suffering when you looked death full in the face and refused
to retreat.

Jesus, empty and alone in Gethsemane's night,
yet full of compassion for us in our need,
walk with us to the very edge of our despair.
Affirm us when integrity is questioned, self-confidence
undermined. Uphold us when energy is sapped and emotions
exhausted.
Renew our resolve when we are overwhelmed by a sense of
futility. Stand by us when friends or partners are unfaithful.
Watch with us when we know the death of a loved one will
come too soon,
Intercede for us when we can't find the words or the faith
even to begin to pray.

Jesus, empty and alone in Gethsemane's night,
light up the darkness of our lesser Gethsemanes.
Fill up our emptiness with your inexhaustible love.

Jean Mortimer

Easter

Risen

Matthew 28:1-10

Light fills our lives
risen Jesus
on this Easter day.

We celebrate your resurrection with songs of joy, and
proclaim your Easter presence in every corner of your
creation.

Let a new day begin for your world. Let the smallest flower
and largest star announce the news that death is overcome
by life and all things are made new.

Let private grief
and public tragedy
be not ignored;
but, through your Friday pain, be gathered up in your eternal
victory as mercy and compassion win, and peace receives
the prize.

Let each of us, no matter what our age or skill, leave all our
burdens at your empty tomb; and, from this dawn
begin a resurrection journey, a pilgrimage of joy
that starts and ends in worship; for you are worthy to receive
all blessing, honour, glory and power for ever and ever. Amen.

David Jenkins

Easter

Joy

John 16:19-33

Thanks be to you
Father of our Lord Jesus Christ
for nothing in all creation can separate us from your love;
sorrow is turned to joy and night is turned to day.

Thanks be to you
Father of our Lord Jesus Christ
for your covenant of peace has not been taken from the earth;
your promises have been fulfilled and you have not forgotten
your people.

Thanks be to you
Father of our Lord Jesus Christ
for all things are brought to life in him; death and evil are destroyed
for ever, and no one can take away your joy from us.

We praise you

that joy fills the earth
and tumbles into newborn lives as people hear the Easter news
and respond in thankfulness.

We praise you

that joy still wins new victories where people trust you with their
grief and cling to you in pain.

We praise you

that joy remains
when Christ seems far away
and gifts of faith and hope from you sustain his persecuted friends.

We praise you

that joy transcends
the deep divisions in our world
and then becomes a cherished gift
to those who do your reconciling work.

David Jenkins

Easter

Genuine Glory

John 20:1-10

Living God
who brings light out of darkness, hope out of anguish, birth out of death, we adore you for your Easter glory.

Mighty God
who overcomes the powers of hatred and evil, and holds the keys of life and health,
we adore you for your Easter victory.

Eternal God
who promises us life abundant and who intends never to leave us or forsake us,
we adore you
for your Easter presence.

Glorious God
who wills that the earth be filled with your glory, and the nations honour and worship you,
we adore you
for your Easter splendour.

Loving God
who understands our grief,
and is moved by our loneliness and guilt,
we adore you
for your Easter forgiveness.

Jesus our Lord
we greet you this joyful day and run to tell the world that you are risen among us.

David Jenkins

Easter

'Woman why are you weeping?'

John 20. 1-18

I am weeping because I am woman, woman who has been used.
All my life men have looked at me and seen only my body.
None of them ever wanted me for myself.
Oh, it isn't all sex:
some just wanted to be held in human arms and hugged
as they never have since they were babies.
But I am more than just a body,
I have experiences to share, ideas to debate, jokes to tell,
and stories that tell of the human condition.
I am weeping as a woman because the men I meet do not understand.

I am weeping at the tomb of Jesus
because when he died, there went the one who did understand,
a man, who treated me as a person, with him I could stand upright,
be myself, and not be afraid.
I weep because I do not know where I can find him anymore.

I am weeping because I am woman,
and I have given birth to every child.
I see them starve,
I see them born to failure and trained to expect it,
I see their ears tuned to hate and their hands turned to violence;
I see their bodies abused for adult pleasure, and their minds twisted
by adult greed.
Across the centuries I have walked
over the battle fields of the earth
picking up the bleeding bodies of my sons,
and in the shattered houses laid waste by bombs
I have found my daughters dead.

I am weeping at the tomb of Jesus
because he was the one who showed us that it need not be so.
With him I hoped that love was possible, that care was real,
that peace could come.
And he is dead. I do not know where to find him anymore.

Mary! Mary!
I am not dead. I am alive and with you.

Graham Cook

Easter

Shalom

John 20:19-29

Jesus, stand among us.
Break down the doors of doubt
and speak your word of peace.

Speak peace to those who doubt the victory of good:
families who have tasted the bitterness
of tragedy;
peoples who have never known freedom
from the yoke of domination;
individuals who have received nothing but opposition
to their overtures of peace.

Speak peace to those who doubt there is a future for the
world: arms negotiators who see little or no progress; peace
women and men who see nothing but
futile escalation;
towns and villages which hear nothing
but the stamp of soldiers' feet.

Speak peace to those who doubt they are forgiven:
those weighed down by guilt of long ago,
tormented by vivid memories of anger and hate;
those who seek escape in drugs
and refuge in forgetfulness;
those families divided over trivial incidents
or more deep-seated conflict.

Easter

Speak peace to those those
who doubt you are alive:
who have been hurt by Christian narrowness;
who are afraid of death;
who are surrounded by scepticism;
those who feel weak and inadequate.

Jesus, Lord and God
by your risen power
dispel our doubt and fear
and we will be your children of peace.

David Jenkins

Easter

Peace be with you

Luke 24:36-43

Christ, who stood among the disciples, showing them your hands and feet to take away their doubts, we welcome you.

Christ, who met with the disciples, eating in their presence to make them see, we welcome you.

Christ, who spoke to the disciples, opening their minds to reveal God's promise, we welcome you.

You,
who stand among us, meet with us, speak to us, have mercy on us.

If we are ruled by doubt, have mercy on us.
If we live in fear, as if you are still dead, have mercy on us.
If we fail to be your hands and feet, have mercy on us.
If we read scripture, but do not grasp the gospel, have mercy on us. If we do not forgive as we are forgiven, have mercy on us.

(Silence)

We receive the gift of grace, from him who promised grace.
We receive the gift of peace, from him who promised peace.
We receive the gift of life, from him who died and lives again.
Thanks be to God.

Francis Brienen

Easter

Food for thought

Luke 24:13-35

It was the breaking of the bread that did it: that's when
I recognized him.
He had said,
'Every time you do this,
you will remember me.'
And we did.
He was there.

I suppose that's what it means, this word, 'remember',
it's the opposite of 'dismember'.
Instead of taking apart
it's putting back together again.
He, taking bread and saying it was his body,
tore it apart and said
that every time we did that
we would remember him.
And we did.
As soon as the bread was broken
I saw his broken, bleeding body
and celebrated his victory.

But that's alright for me.
I will go on doing this,
and seeing him,
until the last breath leaves my body.
But is it enough, this breaking bread?
Can those who never knew him see him in this?
Or does it become just another ritual?

I recall he said, 'You do this.'
And he said it as he was breaking the bread which he said
was his body.
Did he mean that I was to do this with mine? Sweat blood,
exhaust the flesh, serve others till it hurts?
It is not the breaking of the bread that saves but the
breaking of the body.

Graham Cook

Easter

Generous God,
summoning the whole world to sit at your banqueting table,
serving rich food and full-bodied wine for everyone's
enjoyment, thank you for the extravagance of your self-giving
which satisfies the most gnawing hunger and slakes the
deepest thirst.

Hospitable God,
calling all who will share your sorrow and suffering
to celebrate the wedding feast of the lamb that was slain,
thank you for the gracious persistence of your invitation,
which begs the question of our response.

Welcoming God,
coming to meet us along the road,
patiently bearing our dullness, disbelief and self-indulgent
despair, thank you for the open-handedness of all that you
offer to us as guest and host at every meal.

Forgive us our hurried, inhospitable lifestyle
of fast food and take-away snacks,
which takes the edge off appetite
without satisfying our need for conversation and
companionship. Forgive our reliance on instant, convenient,
flavourless eating, which keeps life bland and easy to digest.
Give us the stomach to sit at your table,
to eat, drink and share till all are replete.

Jean Mortimer

Easter

The Road to Emmaus

Luke 24:13-35

Friend who walks our way, before the day is over change the focus of our seeing and help us to be aware of your presence.

Friend who walks our way, before the day is over capture our hearts and minds and help us to hear you in the voices of unexpected people.

Friend who walks our way, before the day is over show us the path to follow and help us to support those who have lost their way.

Friend who walks our way, before the day is over, fill us with your love and may your reflection be seen in us as we break bread together.

Friend who walks our way, before the day is over, make yourself known to us and we will sing your praise and shout with many voices: Hallelujah, our God reigns.

Francis Brienen

Ascension

Breaking the Barriers

Acts 1:1-14; Philippians 2:5-11

What does Christ's Ascension mean? That he is taken away
from us? No, it means that he is given to us more fully. Christ,
crucified and risen is set free-
from one time
for all times
from one community
for all communities
from one sex
for both sexes
from one culture
for all cultures
from one world
for all worlds
from life as one individual
for life within every trusting heart.
Christ at the fireside, Christ at the mealtable, Christ at the
workbench
help us, as we feel you near,
to know how far you stretch your hands.

Christ of the round earth, Christ of the arching sky, Christ of
the furthest star
in your vastness and your power
help us to touch you close at hand.

Christ in the hungry child, Christ in the exploited girl, Christ in
the redundant man
help us, seeing you in need,
to see you, too, in giving hands.

Christ of the deepest depths
Christ exalted to the heights
Christ, both slave and King of Kings; in your manhood, we find
God; in your Godhood, humankind.

Kate Compston

Pentecost

Come Holy Spirit

Genesis 11:1-9; Acts 2:1-11

Spirit of God
as a cool refreshing breeze moves across a sultry lake,
bring our stagnant souls to life.

Whisper your welcome word of encouragement to a world
which needs your presence: a promise that we are not alone.
not orphans,
not left to our own resources.

For you are the source of the power and peace which we have
rejected yet which holds the key to our future.

You are the one who joins us one to another,
the one who reconciles us to our neighbours,
the one who guides us into the way of Jesus Christ.

Come, Holy Spirit,
Heal the babbling brokenness of the world
by creating a new people, international, obedient,
committed to proclaiming your truth, your peace, your life.

Come, Holy Spirit.
Abide in us so completely
that we turn back from our futile attempts to make a name for
ourselves, delighting rather in proclaiming your name,
glorious for ever and ever.

David Jenkins

Pentecost

The Gifts of the Spirit

*A prayer based on Galatians 5:22
and the Lord's prayer*

Come, Holy Spirit, bring us love
and may we know our Father who is with us.

Come, Holy Spirit, bring us joy
and may we honour your name in all we do.

Come, Holy Spirit, bring us peace and may we show the kingdom.

Come, Holy Spirit, bring us kindness
and may we share each day our daily bread.

Come, Holy Spirit, bring us goodness and may we walk away from sins.

Come, Holy Spirit, bring us patience
and may we forgive every one who does us wrong.

Come, Holy Spirit, bring us self-control and may we resist every temptation.

Come, Holy Spirit, gift us yourself
and may the kingdom, the power and the glory come to life in our living. Your will be done.

Francis Brienen

Pentecost

Kindle a flame

Matthew 12:14-21

Come Holy Spirit,
come fire of love,
warm the earth with your touch, cleanse the polluted waters
of creation, restore balance, bring healing, pour out energy,
lighten skies darkened by our sin.

Come Holy Spirit,
come renewer of life,
nourish the potential in us all.
In our work and in our leisure,
waken us to fresh possibilities.
In our family and community life, nurture and inspire our
creativity in all things.

Come Holy Spirit,
come wind of God,
whisper your tender words of healing in the ears of the sick,
breathe your spirit of comfort around those who mourn, stir
hearts hardened by despair to new life and hope.

Drive us out of our spiritual ghettoes to glimpse new ways to
witness, new ways to use our wealth, new ways to work for
peace, new ways of being the people you call us to be.

Come Holy Spirit
Renew the whole creation

(The Iona response *Kindle a flame* Rejoice & Sing No. 393 could be
used as a response after each petition)

Kate McIlhagga

Pentecost

Ephesians 3:14-21

As the earth
is battered and caressed by the winds of heaven, so may your Church great God be shaken and sustained by the breath of your Holy Spirit.

Blow through every Christian fellowship - sweetening rooms where outworn traditions have left a mustiness; where old prejudices have left dust; where lack of imagination has threaded heavy cobwebs from wall to wall.

Teach us that the safe atmosphere of 'good order' must sometimes give way to the gale of new and unpredictable demands on our understanding and energies.

Teach us that your singing wind cannot be caught and controlled within our limiting words and neat dogmas.

Give us your creativity -
to soar on the wings of your wind, light and buoyant,
filled with heaven's breath.

Kate Compston

Trinity

Community

Matthew 22:34-40

Father - Son - Spirit
how hard it is for us to understand your loving community in which one is three, and three is one.

For we, who take delight
in setting up meetings for this and that, so seldom truly meet; nor find the fellowship that dissolves our defences and makes us one with our brothers and sisters.

Teach us to seek out the community of human minds; so that our ideas for creating more peaceful societies and a fairer world may be shared and tested in unity of intent and in the offering of our own lives.
Bring our minds closer to your great Mind.

Teach us to seek out the community of human hearts; so that our compassion - for both victims and perpetrators of hurt and hate and hopelessness - may join with your love in redeeming the world from despair and the abyss.
Bring our hearts closer to your great Heart.

Teach us to seek out the community of human spirits; so that our faith in you and in one another may inspire all with new visions, challenge all to new tasks, reconcile all in a new humanity, and guide all into fellowship with you.
Bring our spirits closer to your great Spirit.

Kate Compston

The Church

House of God

1 Kings 8:22-30; John 2:13-22

Dear God
what is your house like?
Is it like the ones I used to draw with windows in the corners
and brightly painted door?
Do you live in self-detached glory with wall-to-wall comfort
and joy and furniture of dazzling light with not a moth or rust
in sight?

Dear God
what is your house like?
is it like the one they showed me when I grew up tall and
childhood went its speedy way? A house with bells and spire
and pews and musty music from the choir, a place with walls
that last for aye and straw-filled crib on Christmas Day?

Dear God
what is your house like? I read the Gospel and there I see a
man who had no place to lay his head; a man whose home
became a cross
then three days in a borrowed tomb;
a man in whose torn flesh and bone
you came and lived and made your home.

Dear God
now this I know:
your home is neither heavenly mansion in the skies nor temple
made with wood and stones; it is a bread and wine
community, the friends of Jesus in the world, a house of faith
and hope and love.

David Jenkins

The Church

The Word

2 Timothy 3:14-17

Almighty God, we thank you
for the story of your pilgrim people. Through myth, poetry
and prophecy, law and wisdom, gospel and epistle, we witness
their recognition of your nature and purposes slowly
unfolding and gaining ground.

Heavenly Father, we thank you
for the record and promise
of your relationship with humankind. Thank you for the great
shout of faith that sounds from Scripture's pages, and for the
new perspective its truths offer to us on the whole of life.

Lord Christ, we thank you
for addressing us personally today
through the words of the Bible.
Thank you for searching our hearts and minds, sifting our
purposes and thoughts, so that lives can be changed and we
can be brought to a direct encounter with you - who are the
living Word.

Gracious Spirit, teach us
a real love for the Bible.
Show us how to take it
out of its dust jacket
and into our hearts and souls;
how to carry it joyfully
from the lecterns and pulpits of our churches back into the
wide open spaces of your everyday world.
Guide us on the great voyage of discovery
it urges us to make
towards the things that are eternal.

Kate Compston

The Church

Healing for Memories

Wisdom of Solomon 3:1-8

God of our Ancestors:
You are who you are.
You are the God of Abraham, Sarah and Hagar, of Isaac and Rebekah, of Jacob, Rachel and Leah.

And we are who we are:
part of your richly patterned family of countless generations.

We remember before you
those who have died in slavery, and pray that all may live in your freedom:
those who have died in pain and pray that all may live in your healing:
those who have died alone and pray that all may live in your company:
those who have died in despair and pray that all may live in your hope:
those who have died in war and pray that all may live in your peace.

For the dead have been refined like gold in a furnace:
may we, like them, shine for you.

The Church

God our Saviour:
You are who you are. You are the Living God, come now and live in us: free us from our slavery to pain-filled memories, which disturb our sleep and curtail our relationships, and lead us into your presence, where the righteous wait in peace and hope is everlasting.

Janet Lees

The Church

Inferior

Luke 19:1-10

Zacchaeus was superintendent of taxes, and very rich ....

Lord Jesus Christ —
Thank you for being receptive to little men and women like ourselves, who try to be big by undercutting and doing down the chances and advances of our neighbours.

Being a little man, he climbed a tree to see Jesus.
Thank you for bringing us back to earth when, in our very insecurity, we try to set ourselves above you, the better to look down on your world.

'Come down! I must stay with you today ....'
Thank you for that hospitality in your heart which asks for the hospitality of our homes when we are strangers even to ourselves.

He climbed down .... and welcomed Jesus gladly.
Thank you that your love
is the Beauty that will kiss
and transform the Beast
in each one of us
and enable us to walk tall.

There was a general murmur of disapproval ....
Thank you for changing us from little people to big people - challenged and expanded not by censure but by your confidence in us.

The Church

'I give half my possessions to charity .... I am ready to repay.'
Thank you for so caring for us
that our hearts are strangely warmed
and we surprise ourselves
by caring sacrificially for others
and wanting to right our wrongs.

'Salvation has come to this house today!'
Thank you for seeking us out
when we are lost -
and finding in our very brokenness
not just hope for tomorrow
but wholeness for today.

Kate Compston

The Church

Praying

Psalm 121; Luke 9:28-42

Father, forgive us that we are often too busy or too lazy to go up into the hills of prayer - to high ground where we might meet you.

Forgive us that when we do carve out a space for prayer we become easily distracted or drowsy and are unaware of your nearness.

Thank you, then, especially thank you
that your grace so often waits on our slowness ....'
When they awoke, they saw his glory ....'

Thank you for that adventure of prayer
by which we can prepare our minds, open our hearts, and clear our eyes to see visions.

Teach us more about prayer.
Show us how to be still and receptive.
Make us childlike in our trust.

Father, we know that to grab at glory, try to possess it, encapsulate it, tame it, is to lose it: it evaporates.

Forgive us that we try to take your kingdom by storm before it is time. We try to be as God before we have learned how to be properly human.

The Church

Thank you for the fleeting moments when we see your glory -
when our minds clear, our hearts lift and our spirits soar.
But teach us that no revelation is without its 'therefore' ....

.... that, as you show yourself to us, so you are summoning us
into the unlit places of our community and world to share
with others the light we have seen.

Kate Compston

The Church

Christ our Blood Brother

Hebrews 9.11-14

When the people of Israel were on their way from Egypt to the promised land, they had a problem. They had been slaves and now they were on their way to be land owners. They had not liked being slaves and realised that unless they were careful they would become to others as the Egyptians had been to them. They resolved that 'It shall not be for us as it was in Egypt.' They would create a new community, a different type of society.

In the desert they had to learn about the nature of that new community. They had to learn about resources; about freedom and living without slaves; about making fresh starts when things had gone wrong; about caring for the elderly; about the importance of giving both themselves and the land regular periods of rest; about the law and its purposes; about power and how it should be used.

When they had learned these things from God, they made an agreement, a Covenant, with him. They celebrated it by building an altar with 12 stones, they killed an animal and drained its blood into two bowls. One bowl of blood was thrown over the altar and thus given to God. The terms of the Covenant were read out, then, having given their assent, the other bowl of blood was thrown over the assembled people. By the blood of one animal the people and their God were bound together.

The Church

As time went on the people found it difficult to keep the Covenant. The prophets kept on reminding them that God would have justice rather than prayers, and mercy rather than sacrifices. But it was easier to be religious than merciful. Jeremiah prophesied that one day there would have to be a new Covenant. This time the law would be written on human hearts rather than tablets of stone.

The day came when there was a new Covenant. That day was the day Jesus died. This time no sacrificial animal but Christ himself, no altar but a cross. The night before he had poured wine into a cup and gave it to them saying, 'This is the new Covenant in my blood'.

That is the Covenant we proclaim every time we drink it. It will not be not us as it was in Egypt. We will not lord it over others. We will create a new community. That is the new agreement, the new Covenant, the New Testament.

Graham Cook

The Church

God, we praise you for your love for us sealed in blood.
For the saints and pilgrims of faith risking and shedding their
own blood to give their lives for others;
for the blood of the martyrs; God, we praise you.

For Jesus, handing himself over to his enemies
who drained his life-blood with the thrust of a spear;
for the blood of Jesus; God, we praise you.

For the source of our life-blood mothers bearing children
sustaining early life in the womb;
for the blood of mothers; God, we praise you.

For Jesus, carried to birth by Mary, whose blood united him
with all humanity;
for the blood of Jesus; God, we praise you.

For the healing power of blood and all who give it
to restore the health of unknown people;
for the blood from donors; God, we praise you.

For Jesus, loving those with no claim on him
and showing it by giving his blood for them;
for the blood of Jesus; God, we praise you.

God we praise you for your love for us; sealed in blood
flowing through the veins of the body of Christ, uniting us as
we drink wine from the cup,
giving new life transfused with the blood of Jesus;
for the blood of Jesus; God, we praise you.

In the name of Jesus, our blood brother and your son.

Tony Burnham

The Church

Eucharistic Prayer

Hebrews 9:23-28; Mark 14:10-25

Lift up your hearts.
We lift them to the Lord.
Let us give thanks to the Lord our God.
It is right to give our thanks and praise.

We give you thanks, Passover God,
that you have entrusted creation to us,
even though we are disobedient:
that you are God the Liberator,
who keeps a covenant promise with every generation: and that
in Christ our Saviour, the one who was betrayed and suffered,
we have a new covenant for the commonwealth of all.

With all your people in heaven and on earth we sing
Holy, holy, holy Lord,
God of Power and might,
heaven and earth are full of your glory.
Hosanna in the highest.
Blessed is he who comes in the name of the Lord.
Hosanna in the highest. *

Christ of the Last Supper,
despite our everyday betrayals, you continue to feed us with
your body and blood. Hallow these preparations so that,
whenever we eat and drink, whether in city or village, as you
were present in the Upper Room you will be present with us.

The Church

May the Life-giving Spirit give us the grace to examine ourselves honestly, to share generously, and to wait eagerly for new life.

* Could be used with the Sanctus composed by Erik Routley (Rejoice & Sing 13)

Janet Lees

The Church

Bread of Adversity

Isaiah 30:18-21

Stretch out your arms, O King
and hear the cry of your people.
Gather us into the company of your faithful.
Though we eat the bread of adversity
and drink the water of affliction,
may we know your presence
and in faith choose to be one with your suffering world.

Stretch out your arms, O Christ, and bear the pain of your
people. Give bread to a hungry world, the bread of your body,
broken that we might live.
Feed those who hunger for bread and those who hunger
for justice.

Stretch out your arms, O Spirit, and uphold those who faint:
your arm under the head of the weary, your hand to still the
restless, your finger to point the way, your might to conquer
the enemy, your gentleness to rescue the fearful.

Creator, Saviour, Spirit;
Bread created, broken, shared; feed us with your love that
we may be manna for the world.

Amen.

Kate McIlhagga

The Church

Rich in Things

Mark 10:17-22

'Good Master ....'
Jesus Christ, rich in love - forgive us our fulsomeness - the way we flatter you with grand forms of address but trivialise what you are, what you stand for, in our daily living.

'What must I do?'
Hear us when, despite our effusiveness and all the outward show, there is something inside us which knows we are falling short and speaks of our need.

'You know the commandments ....'
Remind us of your basic demand that we respect one another, treating our neighbours as we wish to be treated by them, and that we give honour to God.

'I have kept all these ....'
Bear with us if we assume
too glibly or too smugly
that we successfully keep the rules; but, on the other hand,
do not let us pour scorn on the old guidelines.

Jesus looked at him: his heart warmed to him ....
Look at us, look into our souls, and warm to us in our searching: pity our indecision - our wavering between the wish to be free in you and the wish to be free of you.

The Church

'Go sell everything you have, and give to the poor ....'
Challenge us where it hurts.
Tell us that blamelessness is not enough. Show us the cost of true discipleship. Remind us that we cannot love God fully unless we are prepared to give up everything else.

'He went away with a heavy heart.'
Lord Christ, you give us the freedom to leave if we cannot go the whole way with you; but keep us, we pray, in your love and hold us open to the working of God in our selfish and heavy hearts.

'Everything is possible for God.'
Give us grace to persevere in the Way, slowly surrendering the resources we always relied on, and welcoming those resources from the Father which nothing can devalue and no thief can steal.

Kate Compston

Love

Matthew 15:29-31

God, lovegiver,
the love that dares to speak out, the love that listens, the love
found most powerfully in weakness, the love that heals, this is
the love we need and long for; not counterfeit pretty love, tied
with bows, but lasting love; love that's there when the
sweetness has gone; love that endures beyond the barrier
of pain.

Forgive us
for worshipping the idols of perfection,
for failing to see your glory in the vulnerable, for attaching
more worth to the seen than the unseen.

Lord have mercy
Christ have mercy

Forgive us
for being so full of our own importance,
that we cannot do the one thing needful.

Lord have mercy
Christ have mercy

Forgive us
our lack of perseverance
in face of failure, doubt, rejection; our failure to make
connections; between politics and health, economics
and healing.

The Church

Lord have mercy
Christ have mercy

Vulnerable Lovegiver,
Christ, wounded healer,
Holy Spirit, compassionate friend,
grant us love in all its fullness.

Kate McIlhagga

The Church

Experiencing the Depths

Mark 10:32-45

Loving God
your ways are not our ways, your thoughts are not our
thoughts. We want to see you raised in glory: the first and
the last; our champion and hero.

But what is this we see?
You empty yourself
and make your home
not in the heights but in the depths, not in delight but in
desolation.
And in entering the pit of human risk we suddenly find you
at our side.

Thank you a thousand times
for giving up the safety of your glory
in order to be fully with us in Jesus. Thank you from the
depths of our being for displaying your unselfish way to a
world obsessed by status to a church longing for success and
to individuals absorbed in self-fulfilment.

When we clamour for expensive seats
in the Kingdom,
remind us once more of your throne of glory outside the city,
in the place of the skull, where your miracle of salvation
took place.
And lead us towards that perfection made authentic in
suffering to the glory of Jesus Christ.

David Jenkins

The Church

Jesus, Friend of Outcasts

Mark 2:13-17

Albert was a well known minister in Holland.
He was asked to conduct a major ecumenical service for
Easter in the largest church in Amsterdam.
He looked round for some way of trying to convey the thrill
and excitement of Resurrection.
He hit upon the idea of a trumpeter improvising
on the theme of Resurrection.
Improvisation was important: it was about rising from the
dead. He tried the major orchestra in the city but the
trumpeter there would not think of sinking to improvisation.
So, on the advice of one of his younger church members,
he went to a night club and found a genius of a trumpeter.
The man agreed to play.

On Easter Sunday he did indeed play.
Starting from a low, groaning note he built it up to an
almighty crescendo of sound. They had never heard anything
like it before. It was moving, wonderful and magnificent.
Later that week Albert went round to pay the man.
'Who were those people in church on Sunday?', the man
asked, 'Unlike the people here, they listened, they appreciated,
they understood.'
Albert explained that these were the people of God at
worship. 'Tell me more', said the man,
'I don't know anything about all this.'
They met three or four times.

The Church

They talked about the Gospel, about God and about Jesus,
they talked about the promises and the demands of God.
'I think I would like to be baptised', said the man.

Albert told the story to the Elders meeting.
'Wonderful', they said,
'But he will stop playing his trumpet in that nasty night club,
won't he?'

Graham Cook

The Church

Jesus, what do I do?
I know my ways were not always honest or trustworthy, that
I cheated a bit sometimes; but I've put all that behind me now.
I came when you called and I'll try my best to do things
your way.
But its my friends!

Jesus, what do I do about my friends?
I can hear the mutterings behind my back.
The teachers of the law say you shouldn't be here eating
with me and my friends.
Virtuous people call them sinners
- they never wear the right clothes
- they have no job or do the wrong one.
But I can't throw them out. They're my friends!

Jesus, forgive me if I'm wrong
if they shouldn't be here.
But they wanted to meet you too.
You didn't go away when they came in: you sat at the
same table, ate the same bread, drank the same wine.
Does that mean that despite their faults you'll be their
friend too?

Jesus said: "I came not to call the virtuous but sinners".

Muriel Garrow

The Church

Being Shepherds

Ezekiel 34:7-15; 1 Peter 5:1-11; John 10:7-18

Shepherd God,
your people are wandering like sheep on the open fell:
teach us to gather rather than scatter.
We have failed to lead your people:
teach us your gentle way of honest pastoring.
We cause others to stumble and fool only ourselves:
teach us your humble way of obedient pastoring.

Good Shepherd,
your risky pattern of leadership is not like our romantic shepherd images: help us to be open to your real leadership challenge.
Your people aren't like cuddly little lambs and the world isn't painted pastoral tranquillity: help us to open the door on its craggy reality.
Pastoring each other is a struggle which we find easier to abandon to the few: help us to be mutually encouraging.

Shepherding Spirit,
where we feel compelled to lead by coercion, restore our willingness to be led in obedience: where our honourable motives are obscured by sordid gain, support our eagerness to follow your way: where old habits lead us to lord it over others, strengthen us to be humble with one another: where the people of God seek to lead and be led, keep us from the lion's claws and alert to Christ's example.

Janet Lees

The Church

An unknown God
Matthew 5:13-16

Father,
somebody this week told me they worshipped their
grandchildren. I know what they meant but it set me
wondering about the naturalness of worship.
We're all doing it in some way, whether it's our bank balance
or our football teams.

How can we drag the searchlight back to you, Lord?
How can we witness to your presence with the enthusiasm we
give our earthly heroes?

Show us how we can still enjoy life and give you pride of place.
Show us how we can enter
the compromising world
of buying and selling,
or raising our children,
of responding to the media
and at the same time put you first.

May we be light
for those who have lost their way
in the mill race of materialism.
May we be salt for those who have been wounded by a
society where the fittest survive and the weak are ignored.
May we be peace
for those who are broken in spirit by the claims of many gods.
May you be recognised through us as the God of one and all.

David Jenkins

The Church

The Way

John 14:1-11; Luke 24:13-35

When all roads led to Rome, you came and walked with us, dear God.

When religious laws stilled human breathing and political oppression weighed hard on ordinary people, you came alongside to calm and comfort.

And whether it was to Rome
or Emmaus
or Jericho,
or whether it is the road to Salford or Saskatchewan, it doesn't really matter, for the journey is now more important than the destination; and Jesus, your Son, is the way, the truth and the life.

Help us,
who journey today
to be confident of his presence. As disciples of old met him in wounded traveller or the breaking of bread, so may we recognise his closeness in daily miracles of sharing and responding.

In a polarised world keep us in the one way of sacrificial love, displayed for all time in Jesus our fellow-traveller.

David Jenkins

The Church

I will follow wherever you go

1 Kings 19:9-21

I leave aside my shoes - my ambitions,
undo my watch - my timetable,
take off my glasses - my views,
unclip my pen - my work,
put down my keys - my security,
be alone with you, the only true God.

After being with you,
I take up my shoes - to walk in your ways,
strap on my watch - to live in your time,
put on my glasses - to look at your world,
clip on my pen - to write up your thoughts,
pick up my keys - to open up your doors.

Francis Brienen

The Church

A Cloud of Witnesses

Hebrews 11:32 - 12:2

Before you, O God,
we remember today the ones who went before us. Not held back by the awesomeness of the task they followed you with tenacity and joy.
Full of courage and trust they went to new places, ready to stand and suffer with you.

Like a cloud of many witnesses they stand around us.

Before you, O God,
we remember the saints of our day,
who do not live by the rigid letter of the law but by the wild demands of faith, always prepared to give more, always ready to be turned inside out, knowing that new ways can only be found through risk and pain.

Like a cloud of many witnesses they stand around us.

Eternal God,
we thank you for the witnesses of all times and all places. May the stories of their lives show us the richness of your grace. May they inspire us to look deep within our souls. May they encourage us to take the risk of faith
and to serve you in new ways.

Francis Brienen

The Church

The Bread of Life

John 6:32-40; John 6:66-69

Risen Jesus,
where else can we go? You have the words of eternal life.

We have listened to the sound of politicians
and the arguments of philosophers;
we have been coaxed by the media
and exhorted in the press;
we have heard the doom and destruction preachers who urge
us to flee the world; but where shall we go?
You have the words of eternal life.

Thank you, Lord
for coming to us
where we are,
not to pluck us away
to some heavenly kingdom,
but to send us back
into the city
into the noise
into the world of
half-baked answers and selfish ideologies.

Thank you for promising to feed us with the bread of your
presence wherever we travel.
And when our bodies are tired and our hearts are broken by
the pain of the world,
we know you are especially close; come near, Lord so that we
may know ourselves to be your body
shared and broken in love for your world.

David Jenkins

The World

In Praise of the Creator

Genesis 1:1-3, 24-31; John 1:1-14

Creator God, let there be light
to remind us that darkness has been conquered
and love has filled the universe
in the face of Jesus Christ.

let there be sky
to draw our gaze in fear and wonder
displaying in cloud and thunder,
rainbow and rain
our dependence upon your overarching care.

let there be sun, moon and stars
to give us an appetite for eternity
and to warn us of the limits of our knowledge and pride.

let there be earth
for us to respect and love as we seek to conserve its energy
and resources for children yet to come.

let there be fish and animals
to be partners with us on the earth
sharing our land, sea and air.

let there be people
who as your creatures have not lost their sense of dependence
and who as creators are responsible protectors of life.

The World

let there be rest
offering us the opportunity
for reflection and worship,
recreation and refreshment
with time to remember that a new creation has been
forgivingly provided in Jesus Christ.

Lord
Forgive us when we go blindly through the world.
Forgive us when we spoil, waste and abuse your gifts.
Forgive us when we forget that we walk on holy ground and
renew our sense of awe, wonder and sheer delight in the
riches of your creation.

David Jenkins

The World

No water there

Jeremiah 14:1-6

The life of even the strongest is very fragile, dependent on the elements and the human impulses of every other living soul.

I have taken your rain for granted;
I have taken it for granted that rain will fall, the reservoirs and wells will fill, the pumps and the purifiers do their work and water pour from out the kitchen tap.
I have taken your rain for granted.

I have taken your earth for granted;
I have taken it for granted that coal will be dug and oil and gas piped across continents, nuclear power be harnessed, winds and tides be turned to good account, to give me energy, to heat and power my home and run my car;
I have taken your earth for granted.

I have taken people for granted;
I have taken it for granted that people will want to love and care for each other and feel they have a duty to the poor and weak, to nourish children and to nurse the sick;
I have taken people for granted.

God of power and love, I stand in awe of your creation in all its complexity. Renew that sense of worship in us all and our sense of mutual obligation. Reaffirm the vocation of all who work in public services and utilities to serve the common good. Forgive my self-centredness and call us all into your new community in Jesus Christ.

Stephen Orchard

They all ate to their hearts' content

Mark 8:1-10

We thank you for our food; for the table laden for a celebration with the rich harvest of your earth; for the plates and dishes brimming over,
we thank you for our food

We thank you for our food; for the bread and cheese by the road-side and the hurried snack on a journey; for the meal-break in the working day;
we thank you for our food.

We thank you for our food; the colour and texture of ingredients, the tang of herbs and the smell of spices, the satisfaction of preparing a tasty meal.
we thank you for our food.

We thank you for our hunger for the anticipation of a meal to end the day, for the work which increases our appetite and our sense of taste and savour;
we thank you for our hunger.

Lord Jesus Christ, you knew hunger and thirst and you fed the souls and bodies of those who came to you in Galilee; give us food and friends to share it at our tables day by day; share with us your concern for the unfed; and unite all in your company who break bread at your table.

Stephen Orchard

The World

Waste

Isaiah 34:8-15

Not only in ancient ruined cities
but in and around the modern city
are the waste-heaps and garbage of our lives, picked over by
the foxes and the crows and the human scavengers who make
a living there.

Forgive us, Lord, for mentioning our rubbish in our prayers.
We would rather enjoy the fruits of creation
and forget about the consequences. Forgive us our polluted water,
our toxic soil and sulphurous air.
Forgive us all the dumped surpluses,
the slag heaps and the piles of scrap.

We thank you for the signs of your forgiveness; for the plants
and trees which colonise even the most unsightly ground; for
the animals and birds who learn to live in secret places in our
urban sprawl and turn our rubbish to good account.

We thank you for those who deal with our rubbish, who keep
our streets and houses healthy; who guard us against poisons
and radiation, or who turn our waste into new riches.

We pray for those for whom the rubbish tip is the only source
of food and wealth, picking through others' leavings in the
search to keep their family alive.

Most generous giver, from whose creation there is enough for
all and to spare, make us wise stewards of the earth's treasure
and generous in our turn to one another.

Stephen Orchard

The World

Abraham

Genesis 22:1-18; Luke 20:9-17

God,
in the name of Abraham,
the father of nations yet unborn
our prayers today are for his children.
Far from being sacrificed on the altar
of obedience to your will and faith in your promises we have
risked them on the altars of greed, violence and nationalism.

We weep for the past, Lord, the folly of wars which have
destroyed families, cities, nations; the blindness of leaders who
have led the world into pain and destruction.

We weep for the present, Lord,
the madness of nuclear escalation;
the polarisation of east and west,
north and south;
the tit-for-tat lunacy of terrorism.

We weep for the future, Lord,
the thought of children born into homes
where hatred is commonplace
and violence a way of life;
the prospect of racial confrontation in our cities and a widening
gap between rich and poor.

God of Abraham and Jesus Christ on this day of remembering
we recall that the heirs of your promises are those who take your
risks for you,
risks of trust, risks for peace risks for life, risks for justice, risks
of faith and works together;
otherwise, you will give the vineyard to others.

At the going down of the sun and in the morning we will
remember this, Lord.

David Jenkins

Remember

Romans 4:13-25

Remember Ypres, the Somme, Mons and Verdun.
Remember the Western Desert, El Alamein, the Normandy
beaches. Remember Dresden, Hiroshima and the Burma Road.
Remember Korea, the Falkland Islands and Northern Ireland.

Remember the courage, the comradeship, the ingenuity, the
spirit of working together for a common cause, the planning
together for a better world that would come with peace.

Remember the call to arms, the patriotic songs, the posters,
the partings which were such sweet sorrow, the sound of the
drum, the skirl of the pipe, the prayer that God would be on
our side.

Remember the carnage;
the colossal, stinking, bloody horror;
the ripped bodies on the wire,
the platoons of which only three out of forty lived.
Remember the widows of sixty years and more,
the old men and women living now who never knew their
fathers. Remember the love that was lost, the wisdom wasted,
the minds that were twisted and the limbs distorted.

Remember the wealth of nations being fired from guns,
dropped as bombs: smashing schools, homes, factories,
churches and hospitals; ruining crops, destroying trees.
Remember the hope of a whole generation
left to evaporate in the sands of a desert
or sink forever in the oceans of the world.

And Its People

Remember this day the children who will die while the world spends its wealth on arms; the young who have no work while others in their generation are trained to fight; the ambulances that will not come while we argue about how many troop carriers we need; the research into disease left neglected while brilliant minds are used to study more effective destruction.

Remember the one who asked us to remember him.

Graham Cook

And Its People

This is the day

Mark 2:23-28

Lord of the Sabbath, your liberated love is not bound by rigid rules; your free spirit is not quenched by the letter of the law. For you, every day is wholesome as wheat, holy as bread.
So we offer you everything we do today:
at work, at rest, in public praise and in private prayer: This is the day that the Lord has made. We will rejoice and be glad in it.

We ask your blessing on those who must work today for our safety and security. Be where they are, and in what they do.
Let them say with us:
This is the day that the Lord has made. We will work and be busy in it.

We ask your blessing on those who will rest today after a hard working week. Let them find time for relaxation, better to face the demands of tomorrow.
Let them say with us:
This is the day that the Lord has made. We will rest and be refreshed in it.

We ask your blessing on all your people gathered today to worship you. Tune our praise to your glory, and our prayers to the pangs of your hungry world. Equip us to see and serve you tomorrow in the places where we live and work.

And Its People

So shall we proclaim with all your creation:
This is the day that the Lord has made. We will rejoice
and be glad in it.

Lord of the Sabbath,
let this and all our days be wholesome and holy to you, for
you are the same yesterday, today and for ever.

David Greenwood

And Its People

The Hidden Riches of the Earth

Job 28:1-12

For the people who mine the depths of earth, who drill the
sea-bed and the desert, the snow-filled wastes and lonely
mountains,
we give you thanks and ask your blessing.

For the people who tend the forge and furnace, who roll the
steel and blow the glass, who toss hot ingots and beat the metal,
we give you thanks and ask your blessing.

For the people who mill and turn and polish, who cut the die
and shape the mould, who draw up blueprints, plan production,
we give you thanks and ask your blessing.

For the people who solder and assemble, and check the micro-
electronic part, for those with spanner, gauge and meter,
we give you thanks and ask your blessing.

For the people who saw and plane and sand, who glue the
joints and drive the screws, who paint and varnish, stain
and lacquer,
we give you thanks and ask your blessing.

And Its People

For the people who monitor the cash-flow, raise the invoice,
pack the goods, for managers and forward-planners,
we give you thanks and ask your blessing.

Creator God, you have given us so many possibilities of
shaping the raw materials of earth for our use and pleasure;
may they be a blessing to us and not a curse because of our
misuse of them. Teach us to manage them wisely, for our own
fulfilment and the benefit of succeeding generations.

Stephen Orchard

And Its People

Say one for me

Philippians 1:1-11

'Say one for me,'
says the soldier in Belfast his eyes alert with cautious fear
and his finger on the trigger.
God, be with all who serve their cause and nation in
Northern Ireland. Open the hearts of all people loyalists and
nationalists, leaders and led to receive your gift of peace.

'Say one for me,'
says the woman in the rice field her back bent with endless
toil, her fingers planting the seedlings.
God, be with all those who slave to feed themselves and their
families. Give to all people in every nation a desire for justice,
that gluttony in individuals and in economies may be
destroyed.

'Say one for me,'
says the safety man on the oil rig, his brow furrowed with
daily worries, his knuckles tight on the blueprints.
God, be with those who are trapped between competing
desires. Forgive our consumer greed giving priority to low
costs and high profits above the value of human life.

'Say one for me,'
said the thief on the cross his body broken by agonising pain,
his hands lashed to the wooden beam.
And God, you were with him suffering a thief's pain and
humiliation. We praise you for being human and sharing our
fear, toil, worry and pain.

And Its People

So God, in the name of Jesus we say,
soldier, peasant, rigger and thief:
grace to you and peace
from God our Father
and the Lord Jesus Christ.

Tony Burnham

For Healing

Mark 7:24-37

Loving God
when people who were ill came to Jesus they expected to be
made whole. now with all our pains and anxieties we pray for
the blessing of your touch ..... Our hearts are heavy also with the
handicaps and sufferings of others, we pray for them too .....

Forgive us for inflicting wounds and diseases
on ourselves and on each other
by poverty, careless accident, deliberate risk and through the
poisons we eat, drink and breathe. Give us strength to break
harming habits, and commitment to cleanse the earth of pollution.

And when our sickness or the earth's seem too much for our
weakness remind us that your grace is all we need.

Loving God
we praise you for the gift of healing through nurses, doctors and
all who minister to the ill in home, surgery and clinic, hospital
ward and theatre. And especially we rejoice that in the Church
where your word is heard and obeyed you give new life for old.

But the praise will be loudest when we meet the needs of those
who are so poor that they cannot speak for themselves, people
who are chronically sick,
mentally or physically handicapped old and frail,
giving them the priority in our communities
they have in your kingdom.
Then there will be a health and wholeness
about our life together,
which will unite our praise and theirs
so that once more, on earth
Christ will be glorified.

Tony Burnham

And Its People

A way with Devils

Luke 11:14-26

We do not talk readily of devils, as people did in Jesus' day,
but we too know that our human personality can be swamped,
taken over, as though possessed

Good Spirit of God
whatever possessed me,
when I blurted out that angry word,
when I slapped my noisy child,
when I chased that erotic dream,
when I resigned out of sudden frustration,
when I thought of suicide
- what possessed me?

Good Spirit of God,
whatever possessed us,
when the crowd shouted 'Barabbas!',
when nationalism became a fever,
when racism gripped our hearts and justice fled.
- what possessed us?

Healing Spirit of God
we pray for all who are in the grip of evil, who in despair
see no light at all, who in addiction find no release, who in
bitterness know no mercy, who in fear cannot love.
Heal, inspire, release, renew,
Spirit of the living God.

Bernard Thorogood

And Its People

When the Heat is on

Daniel 3:13-26

Faithful God,
when the heat is on,
help us to be faithful to you.

When people patronise us,
when people laugh at us because of what we believe, help us
to be faithful to you.

When we face the burning in the head,
the unbearable anger,
the restless tension that makes us pace the room, again and
again, and would divorce us from reason, help us to be faithful
to you.

Loving God,
we pray for others who face the heat;

for people of faith in every land
who are tortured in ways we shall never know.
Help all people to bear true witness.

For police bearing the pressure on the streets,
and tempted to bend the truth for the sake of the team and
a quick conviction.
Help all people to bear true witness.

And Its People

For drivers who need to work beyond the point of exhaustion
and tamper with tachometers to provide for their families.
Help all people to bear true witness.

For politicians who fear that nothing will ever be achieved
unless they speak flattering words.
Help all people to bear true witness.

Bob Warwicker

And Its People

Healing the Lost

Luke 15:1-10

We remember that so many people are lost. Missing persons - the pictures in police stations tell us of those who have left home without trace. The disappeared - those in many countries taken by the authorities and never heard of again. Battered wives and beaten children - hidden behind the curtains and unknown to the world.

Seeking God, so many are lost to us
but not one is lost to you.
Keep seeking,
great shepherd of the flock.
We pray for the homes where there is an empty chair;
a familiar face missing; and no news coming.
Keep seeking, good shepherd,
to restore the lost ones.
We pray for those wandering hopelessly in a cit;, lonely in the crowd; taken in for questioning; far away in a war zone.
Keep seeking, tireless shepherd,
to build fellowship anew.
We pray for ourselves, so often lost
in our busyness, in the confused claims on our lives, tempted by our fears into violent attitudes.
Seek and find us, loving Christ,
and keep us in your light.
We pray for all who share in your seeking,

And Its People

all who respond to phone calls from the anxious and
desperate, those who staff hostels and lodgings in the great
cities of the world, and all befrienders.
In their seeking, may your
love shine and rejoicing begin.

Bernard Thorogood

And Its People

Runaways

Jonah 1:1-17; Hebrews 2:1-4

Searching Love, we pray for runaways.

We pray for those who have to run away, because their parents treat them cruelly, because they are in impossible debt, or because they are persecuted for their faith: may they find life in you.

We pray for those who run away from truth or pain, who will not admit that someone they love is gone for ever, whose agony builds inside.

We pray for those who cannot stand their own weakness, not even long enough to ask forgiveness. Forgive them all, help them to forgive themselves, and help them gently to the place where they will see reality.

We pray for those of us who run away from you, from the challenge of your words, from your demands of discipleship, from your love.
Thank you for your persistence, searching us out with love.

And for those whose running leads to a worse place, who fall into darkness like the belly of Jonah's whale, who fall under the lash of the storm or crawl under railway arches: we ask for confidence in you, that they may find peace and homecoming in your presence.

Bob Warwicker

And Its People

God Our Mother

Mark 3:31-35; 1 Thessalonians 2:1-8

Preparation:

God of Love,
gather in your comforting folds
all who seek you.
When the human race is stubbornly against you, teach us
repentance, and forgive us.
We your children,
tired, dusty and shamefaced,
return to you,
forgiving God.

Intercession:

We pray for the mothers;
who struggle on low wages, in high flats, whose partners are violent, or come and go, whose families "disappear", who have no-one to share the burden, or whose children are nothing but a joy. May they find support from you and your people. We pray for fathers, alone or in partnership, raising children. Give them strength to love.

And Its People

Thanksgiving:

We thank you for our parents,
for the motherhood of the church
which had a part in making us what we are,
for the mothers of ideas
in science and art,
for the mothers and brothers and sisters and children we have
in your community: for all these, who come from you,
God, our mother, we give thanks.

Bob Warwicker

Sleep Prayer

Romans 8:18-25

O Jesus, King of the poor,
shield this night
those who are imprisoned without charge, those who have "disappeared".
Cast a halo of your presence around those who groan in sorrow or in pain.

Protect those whose livelihoods are threatened. Encourage those forbidden to worship. Encompass your little ones gone hungry to sleep, cold and fitfully waking.
Guide your witnesses for peace.
Safeguard your workers for justice.

Encircle us with your power, compass us with your grace, embrace your dying ones, support your weary ones, calm your frightened ones.

And as the sun scatters the mist on the hills, bring us to a new dawn, when all shall freely sit at table in your kingdom, rejoicing in a God who saves them.

Kate McIlhagga

And Its People

Cup of Suffering

Matthew 20:20-28

God of birthing,
God of death,
God of ever present breath,
God of steadfast faithful love,
God in Christ in borrowed stall,
God in child so weak and small,
hear us as we pray:

for those, who bear heavy losses, for children at risk, for those camped out in the fields of despair,
for those without work.

Lord hear us
Lord graciously hear us.

God, mother, midwife, judge, housewife, shepherd, father, friend, knee-scarred king on throne of wood, man of sorrows in borrowed grave, gardener, stranger on the road, hear us as we pray:

for those who drink the cup of suffering, for those who watch over the sick, for those who proclaim the mystery
of your risen glory.

Lord hear us
Lord graciously hear us.

God of birthing, God of death,
God of life beyond the grave,
hold out the cup of salvation, to those who serve your needy world. Save us from tricking ourselves into thinking that we are called to privilege rather than service.

Kate McIlhagga

Healing Tears

John 11:1-44

Dear Master,
seeing Mary weep,
you too shed tears for Lazarus - precious jewels of a heart rich
in compassion.

Thank you that you still weep with us sharing our griefs,
releasing with the balm of your tears hurts we have entombed
and never expressed.

Thank you for the sorrow you share with all who suffer: with
little children
starved of love or food;
with young adults
who cannot find work
or any purpose in life;
with mothers and fathers
agonising over a handicapped infant or powerless to help a
child in pain;
with the old who feel humiliated
by the disabilities of age;
with the bereaved,
the lonely, the deeply depressed, the loveless and unlovely.

Move us with your compassion
for our brothers and sisters.
Through tears shed in fellow-feeling and lives given in
Christlike service, enable us to offer hope to those bound by
graveclothes of despair, so that joy grows out of sorrow.

Kate Compston

And Its People

Loving

Song of Songs 8:4-7; 1 Corinthians 13:4-7

Loving God, I offer thanks today
for our human sexuality.
It is sometimes puzzling, often agonizing, sometimes
frightening, often glorious - but it is your gift for us to accept
and enjoy.

Thank you for teaching me that we can find you in one
another when our sexuality is expressed
in enduring care and respect for our partner, in generosity -
as much desire to give as to get, in tenderness rather than an
assertion of power.

Hear my prayer today
for those who are alarmed by their own sexuality,
for those so isolated or handicapped that their sexuality
is imprisoned,
for those who have offered their love to someone
and been rejected,
for those whose love for one another is furtive
and hedged about with deceptions,
for those whose sexual inclinations bring hurt to others,
especially to children,
for those whose expressions of sexuality are divorced
from love
and are uncaring, ungenerous, insensitive or cruel.

And Its People

Thank you for those whose experience has taught me
that your presence may be discovered
in intimate relationships that are warm and caring between
people of the same sex,
in the new happiness found with another partner after the
pain of divorce,
in the special loving often held out to others by those
who have no sexual partner of their own
as well as in the working out of a joyful fulfilment
in lifelong marriage.

Teach us how to celebrate our sexuality
so that we always reflect your tender love for us.

Kate Compston

And Its People

Teaching

John 3:1-21

Lord Jesus, Rabbi, Teacher,
thank you for reminding us
that until we bring you our darkness
we cannot know your light;
that until we become the servants of truth
we cannot become wise leaders;
that until we are good listeners
we cannot speak with authority;
that until we become willing, lifelong learners
we cannot teach with insight or enthusiasm; that until we are ready to be reborn
we cannot truly mature.
Give us, we pray, a questing spirit
and teach us the lessons you taught Nicodemus.
Amen.

Dear God, we pray for those who teach in educational
establishments and churches all over the world: that they may
care deeply for their students
and draw out their potential;
that they may seek co-operation in learning,
not misuse their authority to force or frighten;
that they may be imaginative and sensitive as they help people
to uncover new knowledge and experience;
and that they may take delight in learning from those they
teach.
Amen.

And Its People

Lord God, give to all members of all societies, we pray, an appreciation of the adventure of learning, a ready support for those in the teaching professions, the will to direct resources into the sharing of knowledge and skills, a desire that the potential of all should be realised -
regardless of age, sex, background or race,
and an insight into the wisdom that transcends knowledge.
Amen.

Kate Compston

Recreated

Genesis 2:4-25

Creator God, always sharing your gift of life, always giving yourself away,
your very method of creating points to the way our own lives can develop and find fulfilment.
We praise you
that we have been created for relationships, that one way of discovering who we are is by forgetting ourselves and relating to others.

We praise you
that we have been created in partnership, woman and man, friend and friend, nation and nation; that all created life reflects your purpose and as you show us the value of animals, earth and space, we discover our responsibility.
We praise you
that we have created to change, that as we reach for new horizons and new knowledge, we realise we also need a new heart and a new spirit: we need to be re-created so that we can catch your vision of a new heaven and a new earth.
We praise you
that we have been created to be one: one with you, one with each other, a promise seen, confirmed and born again in Jesus Christ our Lord.

David Jenkins

And Its People

Family

Ephesians 5:21 - 6:4

Lord of all our loving, all our changing, all our trusting;
we pray today that our relationships and friendships may be
living, growing experiences and that in marriage and family
life a new delight may nurture our commitment to each other.

Where homes are filled with respect and love, and where
parents and children live together
in a spirit of gratitude and forgiveness, help us to be full of
praise to you; for you enable these gifts to grow between us.

Where homes are torn by argument and tension and all suffer
the hurt of broken trust, help us not to judge hastily but to
encourage a new spirit of understanding; for you are the
source of reconciliation.

Where relationships have broken down
and love has died
help us to tread carefully and compassionately
lest bitterness take eternal root
and anger spill over into other lives,
for you are a God who shares our human separation.

Where children are the innocent victims of grown up people's
violence or are abandoned to the care of society, let your
energy and enthusiasm particularly surround those who foster
and adopt, painfully creating life out of death,
hope out of rejection,
laughter out of tears,
for such young ones are a sign of your kingdom.

David Jenkins

And Its People

The Divided Community

Matthew 12:22-32

Creator God
in this beautiful and dangerous world, in which you have placed us, we pray today for all who, in your name, seek to bring order out of chaos, beauty out of disfigurement, peace in the midst of storm.

Where the forces of darkness and fear are mustered we know you are present in power.

Where harsh tyranny
crushes Christians into silence
or floods the country with false propaganda, we know you are watching over your own.

Where husband is divided from wife, parents from children, neighbour from neighbour,
We know you are present, understanding.

You walked this way
when you came in human form. You have known the tension, the heartache and the hurt.

Through the ministry of Jesus
lead us in the real world
where evil has to be confronted
and lights have to puncture the darkness.

And Its People

Stimulate us to give active support
to those who are in the firing line
by prayer, by word, by letter,
greeting them as your children
and encouraging them by our own faithfulness.

David Jenkins

One by One

Luke 15:1-10

Ever-searching God, who values each life more than your
own, our prayers today are the prayers of the faceless ones,
all who are discussed and documented
categorised and stereotyped, all whose first name is not
Bertha or Joe or Samidha but the definite article:
the unemployed, the pensioners, the Asians, the refugees,
the hungry the Palestinians, the handicapped.

We turn to you
because we are frightened by
our callous lack of love,
and we feel helpless
at the ease with which government, industry and commerce
can trample on people's lives.

Forgive us yet again as individuals and nations. Re-awaken
our hardened compassion so that
we can make each person feel precious, vital to your world,
delightful in your eyes. And strengthen all who seek to
champion the cause of minority groups in our impersonal
world.

David Jenkins

And Its People

Healing

Mark 7:24-37

Jesus

your body was broken, yet you touched the lives of men, women and children, making them whole.

Show us once more
the wonder of your nearness, rejoicing with those who rejoice, weeping with those who weep.
Convince us that what matters in healing is not a magic formula, or a special form of prayer, but simply the willingness to enlarge our trust in your presence.

In your compassion, come close to those who cry out in pain, to all who are sleepless with worry, and to any who are physically or mentally wounded.

May your presence encourage
those who nurse and tend the sick, or wait and weep as loved ones cling to life.

We pray for all who continue your healing ministry throughout the world, and thank you for churches and individuals who take seriously and joyfully their calling to bind up the wounds in lives which are torn by ill-health, in communities which are divided by bitterness and in families which are shattered by the death of love.

David Jenkins

And Its People

Saying Goodbye

Acts 20:13 - 21:6

Brother Christ,
how painful it is
to say goodbye
to those we love
and go our separate ways!

We know that persistent nostalgia handicaps us - making it difficult to live creatively in the present.
So forgive us
that lingering look over the shoulder and our thralldom to the past.

Stand alongside, we pray
parents whose children are reaching for independence, men and women on the point of retiring from satisfying jobs, friends or lovers whom circumstances force apart, people who work overseas and their families at home, ministers leaving supportive congregations and congregations losing much-loved ministers, all whose calling or duty takes them from communities they love, the dying, and those who must watch and will remain.

Stand alongside - and go before - all who have to say goodbye, reminding us that you for whom loneliness is no stranger will be with us;

and that everything graciously and completely surrendered to you will be safe, unspoiled by our too-human hoarding; and that you will provide fresh manna each tomorrow of our lives.

Kate Compston

The prayers included in this anthology originally appeared as follows:

From   *The Word and the World*, the Prayer Handbook for 1986
        Edited by Edmund Banyard with prayers by David Jenkins
        pgs 16; 26; 58; 63; 64; 67; 68; 100; 101; 102

From   *The Power and the Glory*, the Prayer Handbook for 1987:
        Edited by Edmund Banyard with prayers by David Jenkins
        pgs 6; 21; 24; 25; 28; 35; 39; 73; 98; 99

From   *Encounters*, the Prayer Handbook for 1988
        Edited by Edmund Banyard with prayers by Kate Compston
        pgs 18; 34; 38; 39; 41; 43; 44; 54; 93; 94; 96; 103

From   *All the Glorious Names*, the Prayer Handbook for 1989
        Edited by Edmund Banyard with prayers by
        Stephen Orchard
        pgs 15; 70; 71; 72

From   *Say One for Me*, the Prayer Handbook for 1990
        Edited by Graham Cook with prayers by Tony Burnham
        pgs 13; 27; 48; 50; 52; 74; 80; 82

From   *Exceeding Our Limits*, the Prayer Handbook for 1991
        Edited by Graham Cook with prayers by Jean Mortimer
        pgs 8; 9; 10; 22; 23; 31; 32

From   *Read, Mark and Pray*, the Prayer Handbook for 1992
        Edited by Graham Cook
        pgs 59; 61; 76

From   *Encompassing Presence*, the Prayer Handbook for 1993
        Edited by Kate Compston with prayers by Kate McIlhagga
        pgs 11; 14; 17; 37; 53; 56; 91; 92

From	*Edged with Fire*, the Prayer Handbook for 1994
	Edited by Kate Compston with prayers by Janet Lees
	and Bob Warwicker
	pgs 42; 51; 62; 84; 88; 89

From	*A Restless Hope*, the Prayer Handbook for 1995
	Edited by Kate Compston with prayers by Francis Brienen
	and Bernard Thorogood
	pgs 5; 7; 19; 30; 33; 36; 65; 66; 83; 86

All prayers included in this anthology have been reproduced with the permission of the authors.

Say One Again is designed by Sara Foyle. The cover is based on the design by Maureen Sporle for the 1990 Prayer Handbook, *Say One for Me*.